Divine Power...

The Anointed Call

Divine Power…The Anointed Call

Copyright © 2013 by Dora Mar. All rights reserved.

Published 2013 by Dora Mar Books

www.doramarbooks.com

Scripture quotations are taken from the Holy Bible,
KJV – King James Version. Authorized King James Version.

Cover design and photos by Robert Gromadzki

First Edition, 2013

Printed in the United States of America

ISBN 978-0-578-12047-8

Dedication

This book is dedicated to God the Father, The Son, and The Holy Spirit...

My family, friends, pets and those that have gone before me...

I would like to thank Robert for his unconditional support, editing assistance, and extending his creative talents graciously for this assignment.

Contents

Divine Power.................................... 8

Anointed Call.................................. 16

Heed My Warnings, My Elect.......... 26

Preface

These are the words of our Lord; these words are not to be taken lightly. This is a book of harbingers from our Lord:

I, The Lord your God have called you in righteousness. Walk in My ways and forsake all others. Have I not spoken to you of these? Then why do you not do them. Time is shortened for your sake. Heed my warnings my beloved.

Elect of the Lord now it is time to wake up from your slumber; you were in a time to "be still" now it is time to act. My manifest power will be released in a way that you have not seen before. Rest assured I will do ALL that I propose to do.

See to it that No man deceives you in these perilous days ahead. Have a repentant heart daily and wait for my instructions. When you received them act on them immediately.

Much more bloodshed is ahead, do not be weary of this, this must take place in order to see my Glory. Your cries have come before me as a bitter sweet ointment. I will write my words in your heart; there they will penetrate deep within you.

Listen carefully to these messages written therein.

May you abide in His perfect love forever! AMEN

In order to walk in The Father's Divine Power, you must first seek Him with all of your heart and soul. You must deny yourself and take up the cross: the persecution of Christ. You must capitulate all that you are over to Him. The Father is calling His Elect to have no other idols before Him and to stop any adulterous behaviors and acts of disobedience. He calls you to REPENT daily.

By walking in His righteousness and perfect will, you are fulfilling the will of the Father. Therefore satan, the deceiver, is furious and will try to deceive you at all costs. For life here on earth is but a vapor. On a daily basis, if you are not experiencing the divine power that Elohim has intended for you in these critical times, then you need to check yourself before Him and ask what needs to be brought to light. Our Father is a jealous God, and He shall have no other gods before him. You must seek out His will in EVERYTHING. He requires this of you.

"And ye shall seek me, and find me, when ye shall search for me with all your heart."
(Jeremiah 29:13)

Chapter One

Divine Power

Chapter One: Divine Power

Our Lord has given His elect divine power to fulfill His work here on earth. We must use His divine power in accordance to His will or we are not acting within His will. The source of power that is not in accordance to His will is demonic.

There are many forces at work to hinder the work of our Lord in us. In order to discern whether or not you are influenced by demonic forces, you need to seek the face of our Lord continually and walk in His righteousness. Ask for discernment, He will give it to you.

Let no outside influence hinder your walk. Our Lord's power is great and will help you overcome the adversary. There are many adversaries and they all have names, however, there is ONE name above all names, and that name is Yeshua Ha Mashiach, Jesus the Messiah.

Call upon the Father and He will answer you and warn you of things to come. The winds of change have come. We as His believers are already seeing the effects of this. Our Lord has equipped us with the necessary tools to do the work He has asked of us. We've already been receiving miraculous manifestations and miracles. I will share one in particular event in my life that happened in 2008. I had been sleeping and approximately three in the morning I awoke to what sounded like someone had just clashed two cymbals together above my head, and I awoke abruptly. Then, as I opened my eyes, I saw what looked like liquid silver. Then as I adjusted my eyesight to what was before me, I saw an orb of bright white light that proceeded to move from one side of my bed to the other.

As I followed this light, I felt an indescribable peace. Even my dog that was lying beside my bed followed the beautiful white light. As I stood on my feet, I asked the Lord, "Is that you? Do you want to tell me something?" I fell to my knees as He said, "Yes, daughter." Then my room was lit up with beautiful lights with the appearance of the aurora borealis. It was magnificent! But even more magnificent was the small glimpse of the Glory of the Lord that was shining before me in my room.

Then I asked the Lord what was it that He wanted me to do. He wanted me to write about a vision that He was going to show me. So I went to my desk and waited for the vision. As the vision began, I saw a very large black kettle with many people gathered around it, for as far as I could see. Then I saw a whirlwind that was swirling around causing money to come out of the pockets of the people gathered around the black kettle. I asked the Lord what was the meaning of this vision. He answered me saying that the kettle represents the one world government. And the money flowing out of the pockets of the people gathered around the black kettle represents the devaluing of the world's currencies which will eventually be combined into a single worldwide economic source. As we can see, we are headed in this direction; the stage is being set right now.

We must be "set apart" from this world and seek to be holy. If you have been given "Divine Power" from the Father by His Ruach Ha Kodesh (Holy Spirit) then you must act in it. Since walking in His truth, the Lord has been revealing more and more mysteries, and His Divine Power within me has greatly increased.

Be prepared when His Divine Power is at work in you, there will be much persecution. Remember that the only power satan has over you, is the power that you give him. The enemy, satan, cannot read your thoughts, only the Father, Son and Holy Spirit can. We can certainly hear the enemy, and we must know the difference between the voice of Elohim (God) and the voice of the enemy. My friend Robert always reminds me that while the enemy cannot read our minds, he can read our expressions and actions. Then the enemy tries to divert our attention away from the truth by observing how we will react when he tries to whisper perversions. Therefore, you should not let your expression and actions show giving in to temptation and defeat. Pray in the Spirit often and worship Elohim and the enemy will flee from you.

Embrace the Divine Power and gifts that the Lord has given you!

Even when you are going through trials and tribulation, fear nothing and no man. This is the refinement that you must endure to be purified. If you have a deep desire for spiritual things, you will be given spiritual things. Therefore, you should never be fearful but trust that your heavenly Father knows what you need and will provide; even when it seems impossible. Do not be afraid to ask Him. For the Lord has spoken many times to me, "Is there anything too difficult for me?" and then I answer, "No my Elohim, nothing is too difficult for you." Remember, this earthly timetable is temporal, but Elohim's heavenly kingdom is eternal.

Our heavenly Father has given us the divine power to search out His truth and find it!

"According as His divine power hath given unto us all things that pertain unto life and godliness, through the knowledge of him that hath called us to glory and virtue". (2 Peter 1:3)

Do not walk in false humility, but be secure in your gifts and convictions as they have been given unto you. But remember to examine yourselves daily, lest you stumble in your own acknowledgements.

When He gives you a word or acknowledgment, ask for the meaning and research this truth. When our Father spoke to me a few years ago regarding Christmas, all He said to me was "You will never feel the same about this holiday again." I heard it audibly and clear. So I immediately asked Him to show me why, and I began to do some research on my own. Along with my friend Robert, I proceeded to research the original roots of the traditions and we were astonished at our findings.

If you have not already done this, please research the roots and traditions of <u>all</u> of the holidays that you partake in, and I am confident you will never feel the same about them again. With this new found knowledge, I needed to act, and show the truth that was now revealed to those around me. Why did Elohim choose now, and not many years ago? I can only say this, His timing is impeccable and I trust in His divine purpose for me.

When explaining this knowledge to my family, my grandchildren gave me this thought from their young impressionable minds: "Why are people scrambling around buying gifts for each other, when it is supposed to be about Jesus and not the people anyway?" I asked them how they felt now that I explained this truth and how I would not be giving them gifts on this day. This was the answer of Adam, Celina and Cianna: "Didn't you always tell us that it is better to obey God than to sacrifice?" We know it will be a sacrifice to give us gifts, so you better obey God."

"Behold, to obey is better than sacrifice." (1 Samuel 15:22)

"Therefore I take pleasure in infirmities, in reproaches, in necessities, in persecutions, in distresses for Christ's sake: for when I am weak, then am I strong." (11 Corinthians 2:10)

I was praying in the Ruach ha-kodesh (Holy Spirit) over my grandson Jonathan one evening because there was a red light lit up near him. At first I thought it was his cell phone light and then he said he did not have his cell phone near him. So I began to cast out the enemy away from us in Elohim's heavenly language. Jonathan told me after the prayer that he saw a white ribbon flow out of my mouth as I was praying and a beautiful blue light essence was all around the ribbon and he saw the words displayed in English. They were words glorifying Elohim, the creator of this divine power!

Chapter Two

Anointed Call

Chapter Two: Anointed Call

What is the anointed call? The anointed call is Elohim's call for His chosen people.

"My sheep hear my voice, and I know them, and they follow me" **(John 10:27)**

The elect are experiencing the perplexities of this world, but He says to them: "Do not be dismayed by all the chatter amongst you, I will clarify all things to you as you seek me with your whole heart. The treacheries of this world will not harm you if you fully trust me and put your faith in me." Hide His words in your heart as a hidden treasure. Even when you think there is no way that you will make it through a certain situation; He will make a way, if you trust Him.

Elohim says, "My true remnants are as diamonds in the rough, they don't falter when refinement comes and they accept my purging within their life with humility and acceptance." Our Father has great plans for those who wholeheartedly trust and seek Him.

As an onion has many layers, we have many layers that peel away and reveal the inner core of who we really are. The inner core is the root of our being. As the layers are stripped away, another layer is exposed. When a new layer is exposed, there are new hardships to endure. If you do not reach out to our Father, you will not be able to bear the hardships alone. The Father is exposing all unproductive seeds, that is, the disobedient and the unfruitful. He is also preparing his remnant for His occasion.

A few years ago, I had experienced a severe automobile accident for the first time in my life. It was a beautiful Saturday afternoon, and I was stopped at a traffic light at a four way intersection. Without notice, I was hit by a large conversion van traveling at a high rate of speed. The driver of the van was on his cell phone and did not even notice that my vehicle was stopped at the red light. I must mention that I did not hear or see this impact coming.

In a moment, I was before the glory of the Lord! I had experienced His presence before of indescribable peace and love, so it was not foreign to me. I saw a bright white light in the presence of Yeshua and I said to him, "Where are all the others?" (I thought I had been raptured). He replied, "No, daughter, you have been in a very bad car accident." I replied, "Who me?" in disbelief, because I did not see or feel anything.

He then said, "You must go back and tell my people that I am coming sooner than they think."

Then, in a moment, I was back in my body which was shaking profusely. I cried out to the Lord and said, "Please help me, I do see that I was in an accident but I can't stop shaking." I saw smoke from the exploded airbags and I thought the vehicle was on fire. I could see that my seatbelt that was torn off me, with my necklace dangling from it. At that moment I felt peace enter my body and I was able to think clearly and assess what I needed to do next as the police and ambulance arrived at the scene. Even though there was glass all around me, I was not even scratched. Another thing I do remember is the Lord telling me that His angels covered me and that I would only experience some of the effects of the accident, but not as devastating as it could have been.

The day before the accident, I was praying fervently to Elohim when all of the sudden I heard Him speak to me saying that I needed a new heart. I was confused because I thought that I had given Him my heart. This was not what He was talking about; He meant my physical heart. Even though doctors have a very specific and special place, I am not one who likes to visit them, so I became very afraid. I knew something was going on with my body that was not right due to the way that I had been feeling. I even had a difficult time walking my dog and didn't know what was wrong. Now I understood why I had all of the symptoms that I had been experiencing. Bless my dear and beautiful mom, she knew something was wrong and kept prodding me to visit a doctor, but I just wouldn't. The words of Adonai literally pierced my heart, as you will find out.

As I lay on my bed, I heard Him say to me, "Don't be afraid, I am going to give you a new heart." I was a little frightened not knowing how He was going to do this. Just then, I felt as if I was slipping into a deep sleep, but before I fully fell asleep, I saw an open vision of Yeshua carrying me up a beautiful stairway with what looked like liquid crystal under His feet. My body was draped in His arms as if I had no life. He was carrying me to the Throne Room of Heaven before the Father.

When I awoke, I felt as if I was waking up from anesthesia. Then I heard the Lord say to me, "It is done." He then said to me that He left a mark on the area to show where He performed this miraculous healing! I immediately went to the mirror to see the mark He spoke of, as a sign that He performed all that He said He would. It was like a small red mark over my heart, and I fell to my knees crying out praising and thanking Him for all He had done! Then I said, "How long will this one last?" And He replied, "About 50 years, but you won't need it that long." Our Lord has such a beautiful sense of humor. I smiled because I knew this meant He would come to get me before then. If I didn't have this new heart, I wouldn't have made it through the accident on the very next day. Nothing is impossible with Elohim, absolutely nothing!

The elect of the Lord are entering into a season of divine power. When you walk into a room, you will emulate the holiness, power and authority given to you by our Father. In the past, His chosen performed miracles in Yeshua's name. In this new season, it will be like it was in the days of old, but even greater!

Remember, many are called and only few are chosen. When your flesh is crucified, you will be hated for His sake.

"Hear the word of the Lord, ye that tremble at his word; Your brethren that hated you, that cast you out for my name's sake, said, Let the Lord be glorified: but he shall appear to your joy, and they shall be ashamed." (Isaiah 66:5)

"For many are called, but few are chosen." (Matthew 22:14)

"I say then, Have they stumbled that they should fall? God forbid: but rather through their fall salvation is come unto the Gentiles, for to provoke them to jealousy." (Romans 11:11)

The seed of faith has been planted within you. So therefore, allow the seed to grow without the hindrances of this world. Be separated, so the weeds will not corrupt the good fruits that the seed has produced.

"Therefore it is of faith that it might be by grace; to the end the promise might be sure to all the seed; not to that only which is of the law, but to that also which is of the faith of Abraham; who is the father of us all." **(Romans 4:16)**

As the seed breaks forth you will know that you have entered into a new season. The Lord desires you to come to Him often and bask in His Holy Light. There, you will be refreshed and nourished. How do you get there? By the Holy Spirit; He will lead you, sons and daughters, to the Most High. Do not panic in these perilous days; don't look away from the Father, lest you will fall into temptation and fear.

Endure to the end and He will give you the crown of life.

"Blessed is the man that endureth temptation: for when he is tried, he shall receive the crown of life, which the Lord hath promised to them that love him." **(James 1:12)**

Each of His chosen have different and specific callings. Some may be called to give strong admonishments like John the Baptist:

"For I say unto you, Among those that are born of women there is not a greater prophet than John the Baptist: but he that is least in the kingdom of God is greater than he." **(Luke 7:28)**

Some may be called to give gentle but powerful admonishments like Stephen:

"And Stephen, full of faith and power, did great wonders and miracles among the people." **(Acts 6:8)**

And some may be called to minister as Mary did:

"Then took Mary a pound of ointment of spikenard, very costly, and anointed the feet of Jesus, and wiped his feet with her hair: and the house was filled with the odour of the ointment." **(John 12:3)**

Some may be called to serve as Martha did:

"There they made him a supper; and Martha served: but Lazarus was one of them that sat at the table with him." **(John 12:2)**

Some may be called fight as David did:

"And David said to Saul, Let no man's heart fail because of him; thy servant will go and fight with this Philistine." **(1 Samuel 17:32)**

Whatever your call, serve Him with gladness, repent daily, and strive for holiness.

"And whatsoever ye do, do it heartily, as to the Lord, and not unto men." **(Colossians 3:23)**

Therefore, be patient with one another. Have the understanding of each other's unique call which is mingled with their personality and passion to serve the One True Elohim.

Chapter Three

Heed My Warnings, My Elect

Chapter Three: Heed My Warnings, My Elect

The deceiver is satan, along with his demons. The name Lucifer is a dead name; Jonathan was given this by the Holy Spirit one day when we were pondering why people are still using this name to refer to satan. When Lucifer was ejected out of Heaven for blaspheming the most High and wanting to be God, his name became a dead name. So when you hear people referring to satan using this name, beware, unless they are telling the story of him from the beginning.

"Take heed to yourselves, that your heart be not deceived, and ye turn aside, and serve other gods, and worship them;" **(Deuteronmy 11:16)**

Elohim keeps saying to me over and over, "Do not be deceived!" He told me on December 12, 2012, "I have heard the crying of my people, but they are disobedient to me." Elect, let us take head to His warnings. He repeats these words so that we understand their importance, as with great provision, comes great responsibility.

"For there shall arise false Christs, and false prophets, and shall shew great signs and wonders; insomuch that, if it were possible, they shall deceive the very elect." (Matthew 24:24)

Each remnant, and elect, of the highest Elohim has a different assignment. Remember to use your time wisely. There is much evil and trickery in disguise running rampant; you must have discernment in everything you do.

When we know that an individual is family through our bloodline, it makes a difference how we look at that individual. Now we are of the bloodline of Christ, which means we have received Yeshua's free gift of salvation. We are now covered by His precious blood and walk in His righteousness. So should we treat one another in Christ according to the relationship we have in Him. Those outside of a relationship to Christ should be treated with caution and discernment.

If the Ruach ha-kodesh leads you to rebuke, then you must rebuke according to the Spirit's leading. If you are called to admonish, then admonish according to the Spirit's leading. If you are called to witness, then you must witness with the Spirit's leading. Yes, this sounds so simple my beloved, but in fact these words are directly from the Father.

He has been observing how we are treating one another and at times He is not pleased. He has said, "Let there be no lying among you; let there be no backbiting among you; let there be peace amongst you; let there be longsuffering amongst you; and let there be love amongst you."

The Lord says, "Some of my elect are perplexed at these words. Be not perplexed by the words I speak to you my elect; I am coming for a true, blameless bride. Don't make my coming back the main focus, but instead purify yourselves for my coming. I long for my people to be deceived no more!"

Many of Elohim's people are worshipping idols unaware. These words are His to His Church: "Regarding paganism in my church, false doctrines are being preached. My people are not taking a stand to defend my truth. Their ways are deceptive and self-serving: only to please themselves and not suffer the persecution of following my ways. This is uncomfortable for many. They would rather not stir up any controversy. I am displeased with the lukewarm behavior in my church. Take a stand, as uncomfortable as it may be. Do you think you please me when you intermingle my truth with lies? This is an abomination to me. Regarding the holidays that you partake in, have you researched to see what you are partaking in, if you haven't, then you need to. If you truly desire to please me, then you will seek me with all your heart and you will find me and my truth of what pleases me."

As you search for truth, you may feel ashamed that you haven't taken the time to research these truths sooner. Believe me, I was ashamed and asked for forgiveness for following blindly in the traditions of men. As the revelations unfolded before me, I felt such liberation in Christ, and even though the persecutions are great, the reward of walking in the righteousness of Christ is greater.

"Elect according to the foreknowledge of God the Father, through sanctification of the Spirit, unto obedience and sprinkling of the blood of Jesus Christ: Grace unto you, and peace, be multiplied."
(1 Peter 1:2)

Shalom!

Notes

Notes

Notes

Notes

Notes

Notes

Notes

Notes

Dora Mar Books

www.doramarbooks.com

www.ingramcontent.com/pod-product-compliance
Lightning Source LLC
Chambersburg PA
CBHW020024050426
42450CB00005B/633